Néjib

my hands

red comet press · brooklyn

greet

touch

say goodbye

ask to
speak

count

write

build

destroy

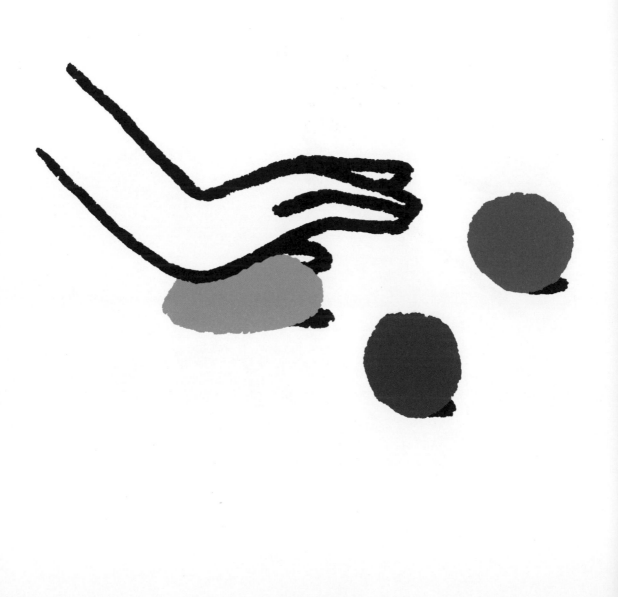

flatten

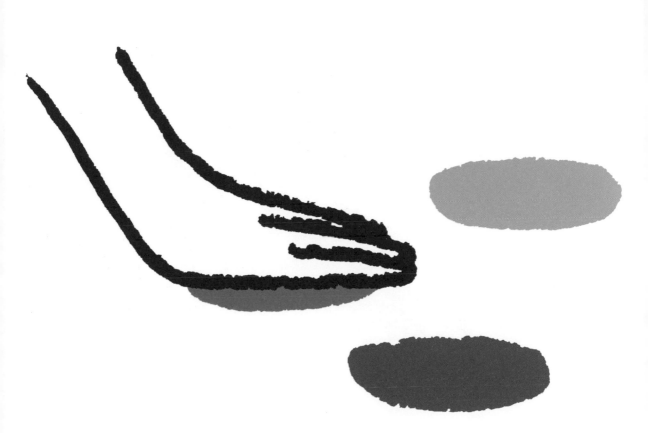

make
tracks

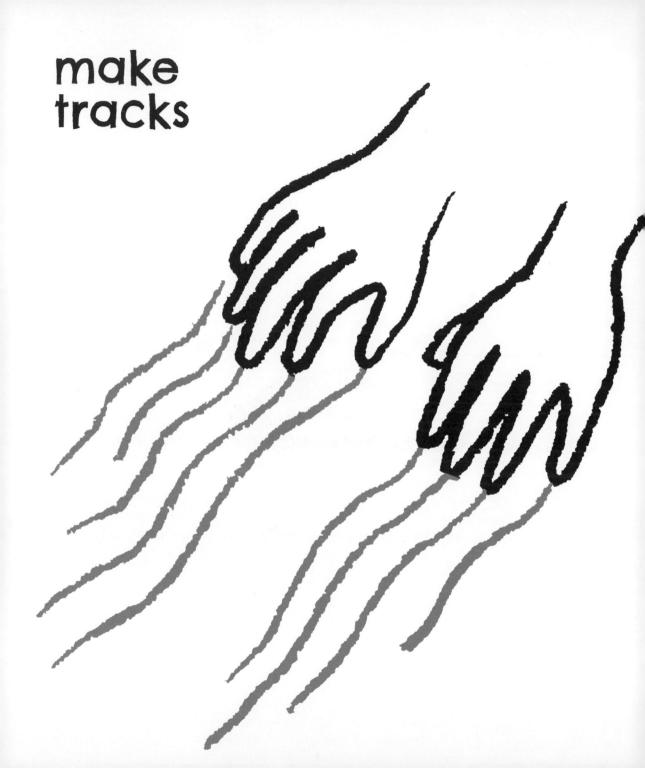

make
prints

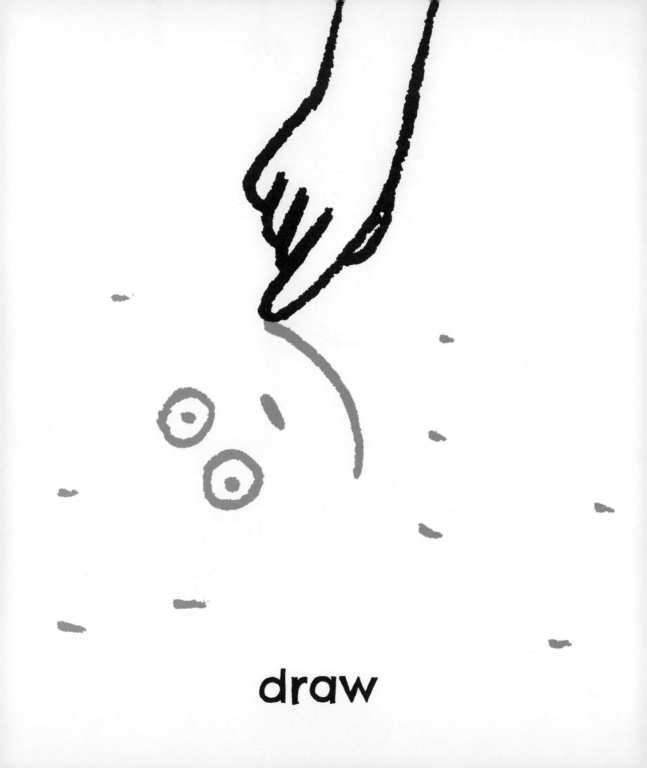

draw

erase

refresh

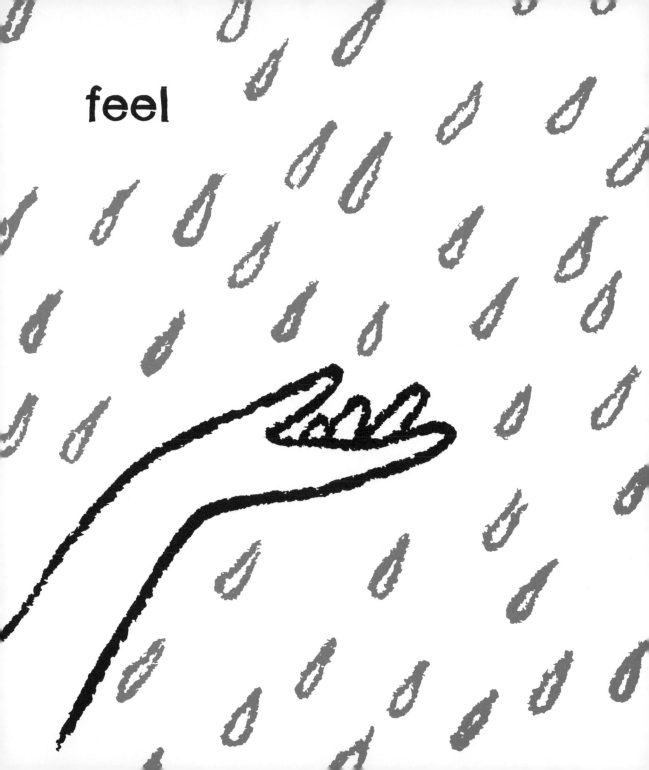

feel

wash

paint

thumbs-up!

make a heart

lift

drive

accompany

nail

hang

throw

catch

victory!

stop!

walk

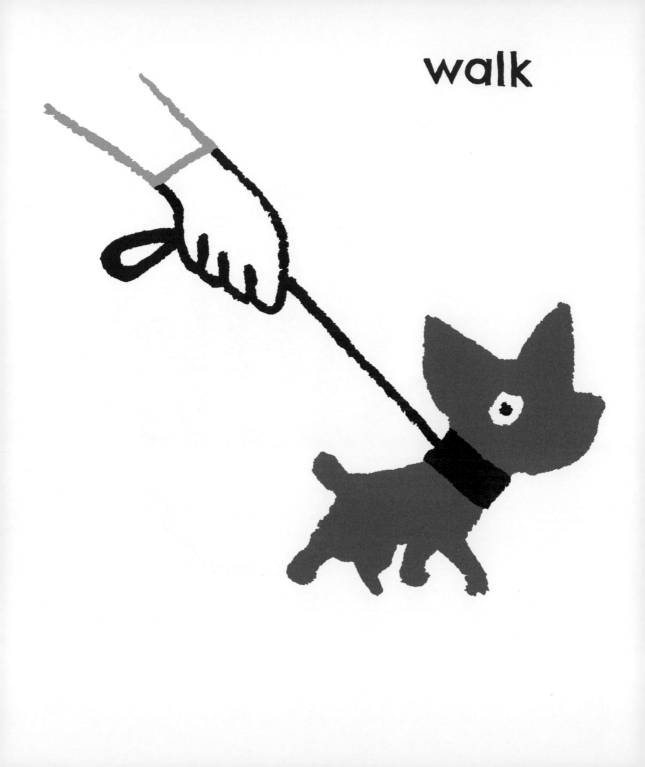

feed

stroke

scratch

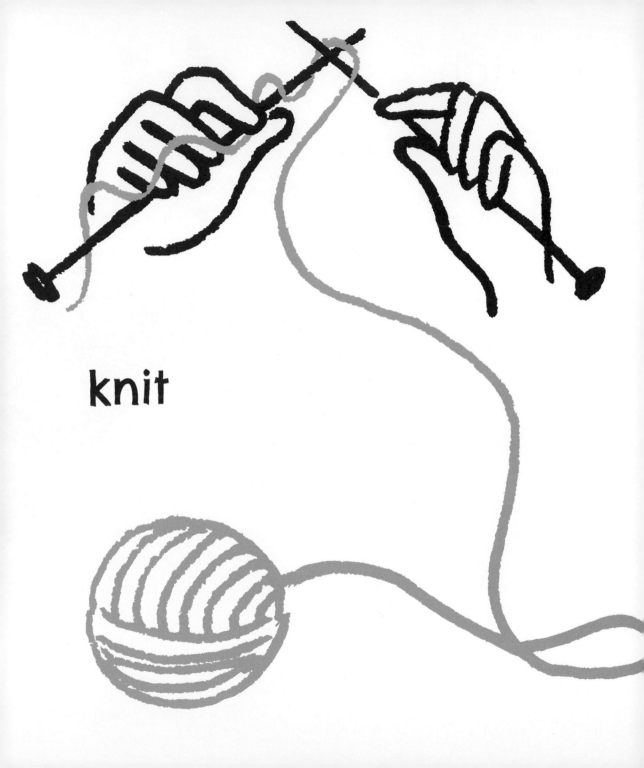

knit

sew

prick

bend

break

repair

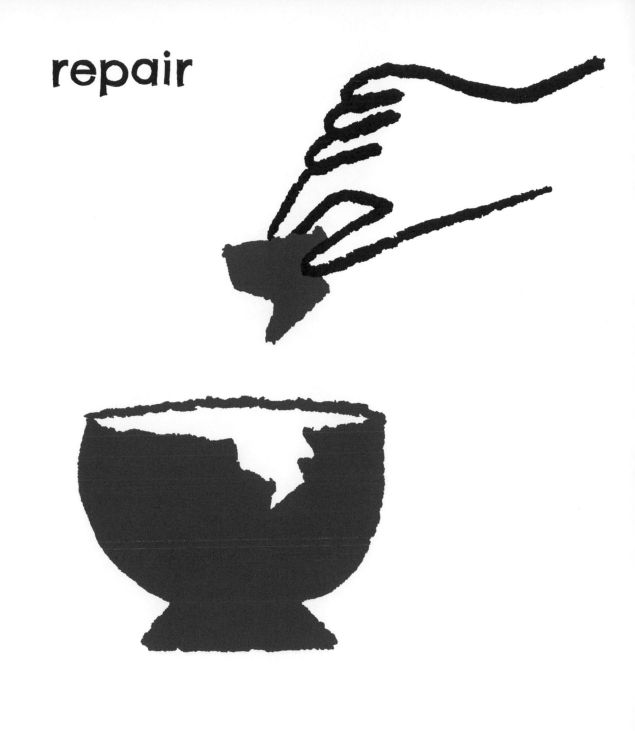

challenge

sulk

dream

make fire

warm up

hide

peek-a-boo!

cover

tear out

collect

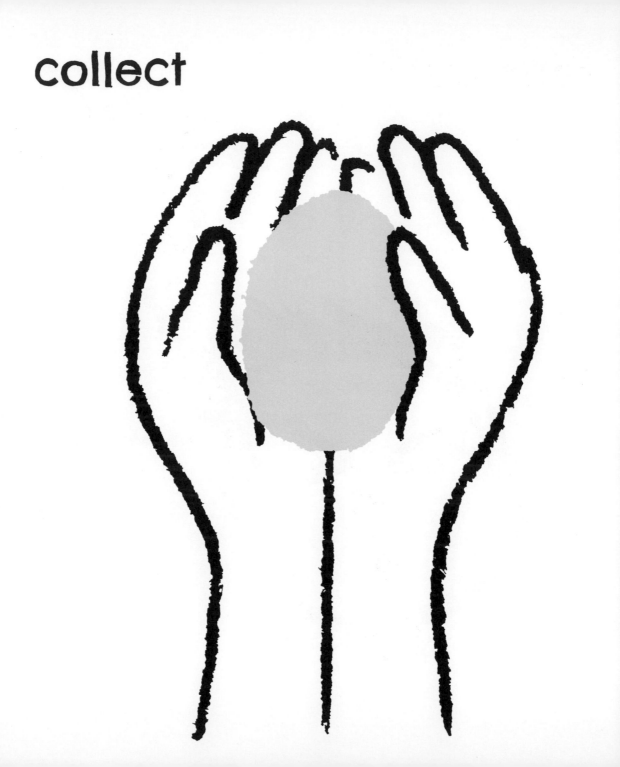

welcome

fish

swim

help

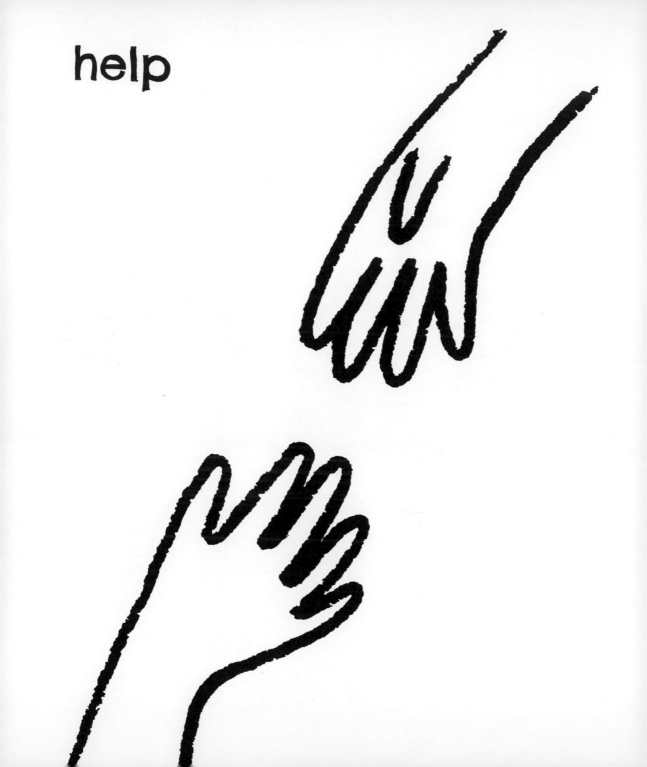

save

pick up

save

put on
a show

light up

knead

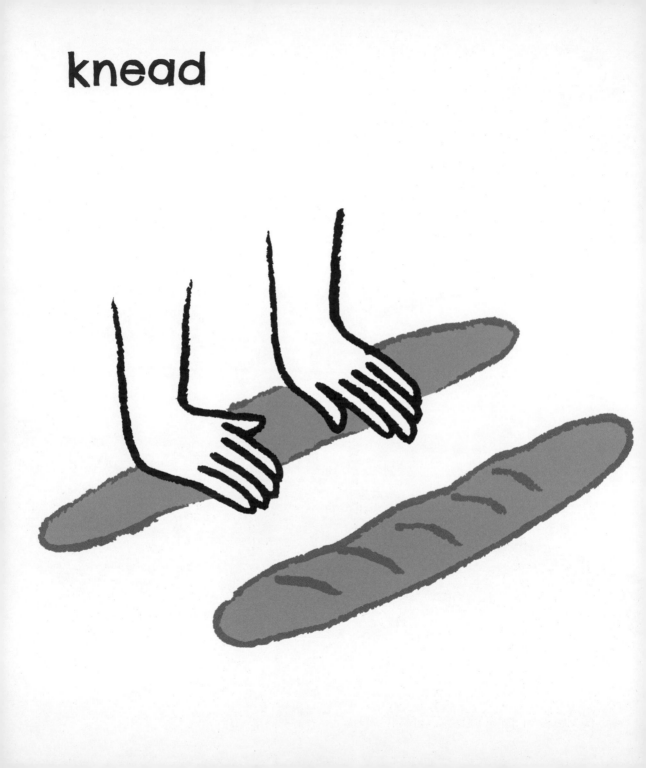

cook

pull

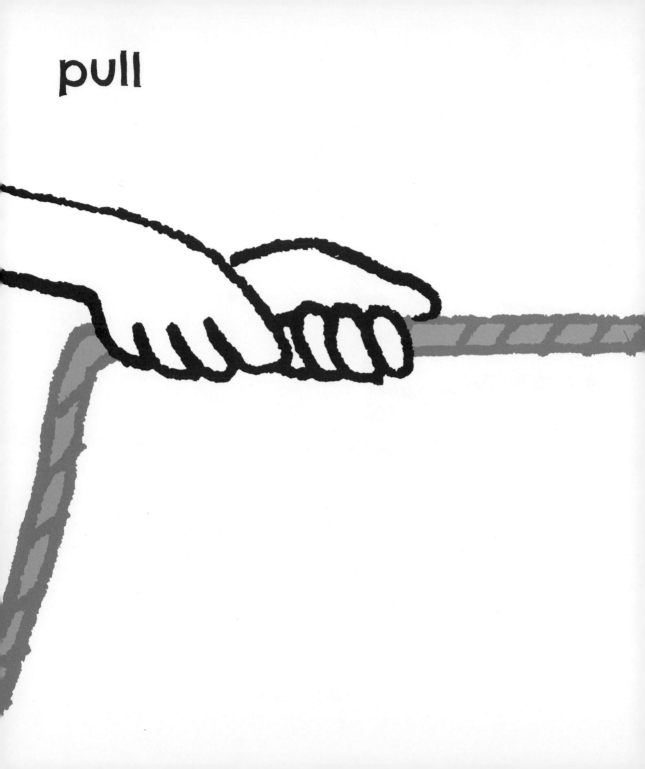

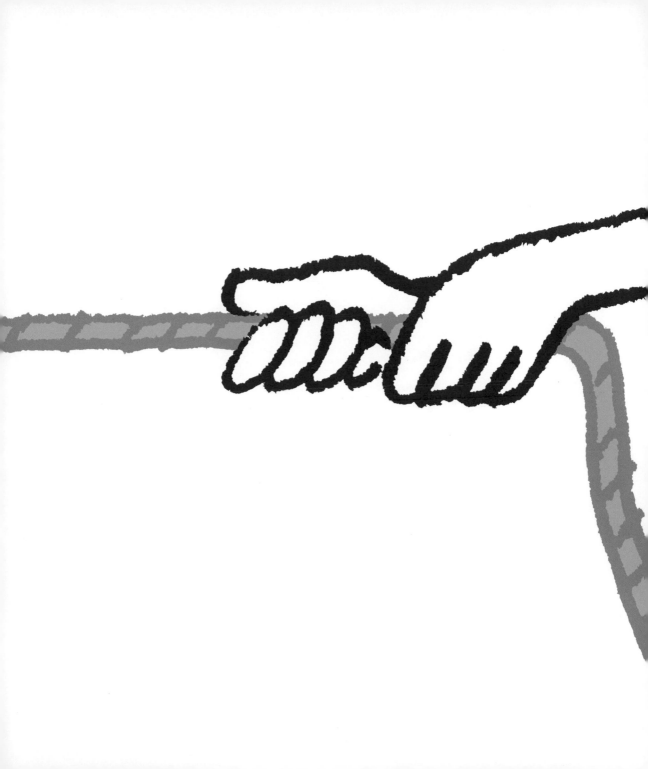

cut

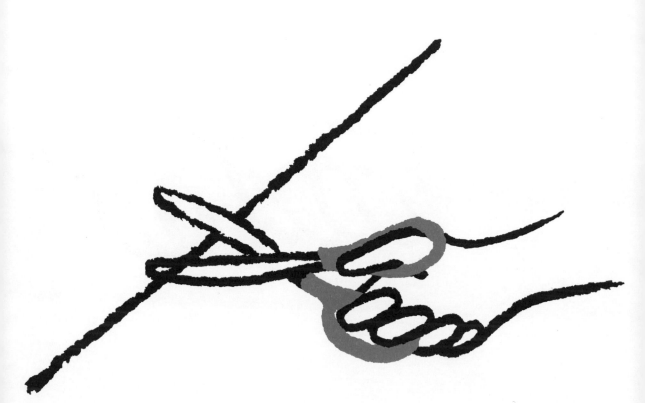

tear

crumple

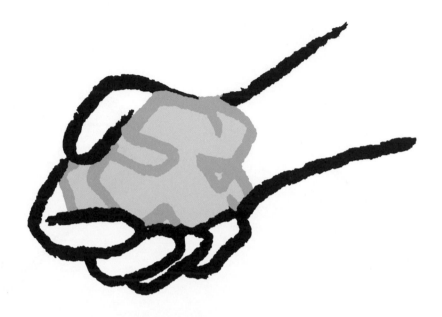

throw away

fill

empty

juggle

decorate

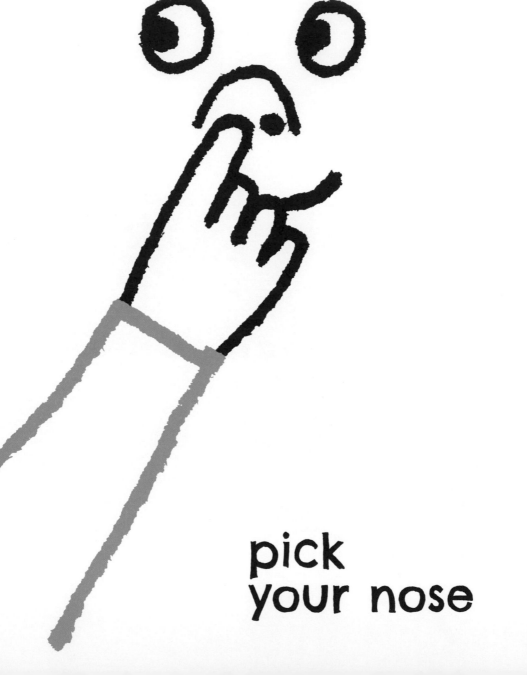

pick
your nose

applaud

tie

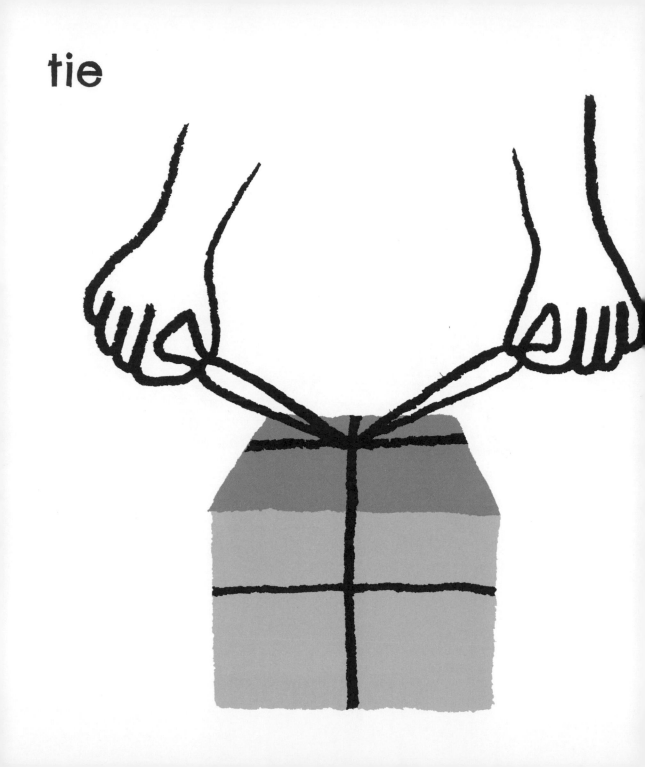

untie

close

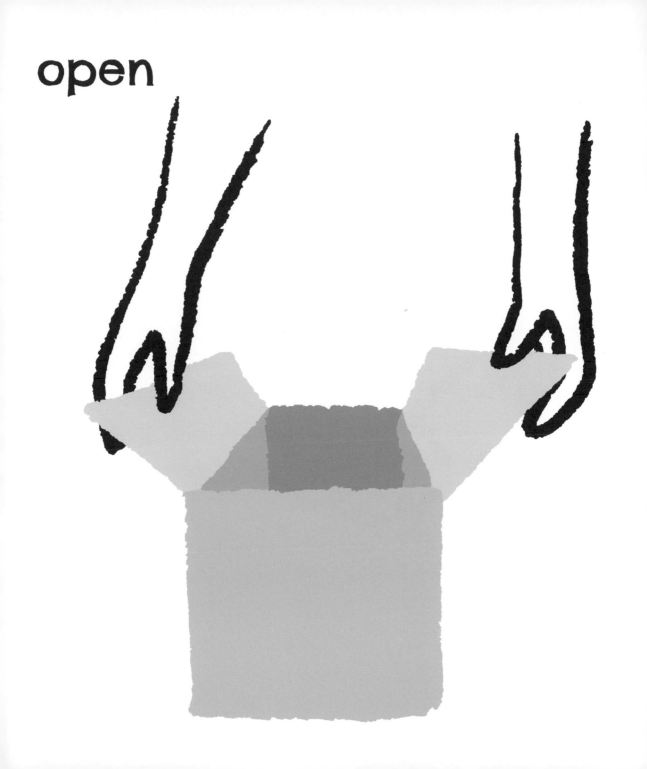

carry

push

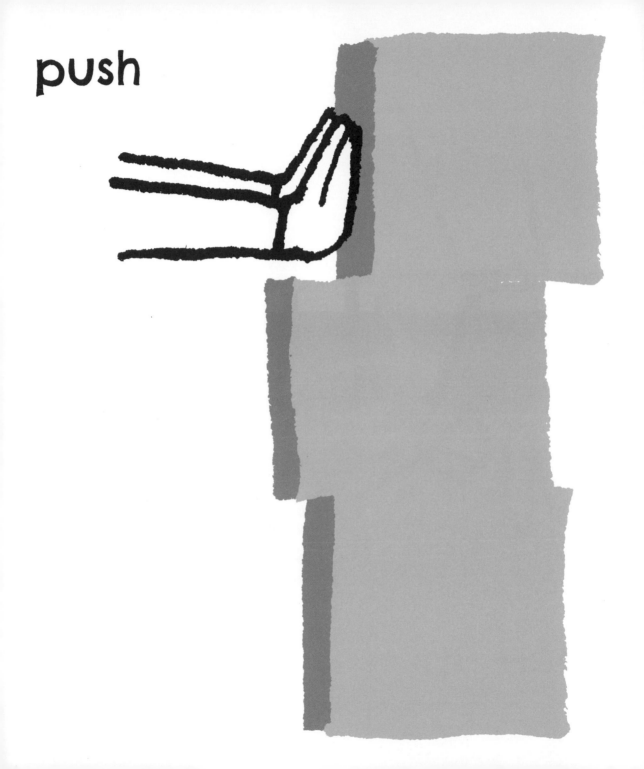

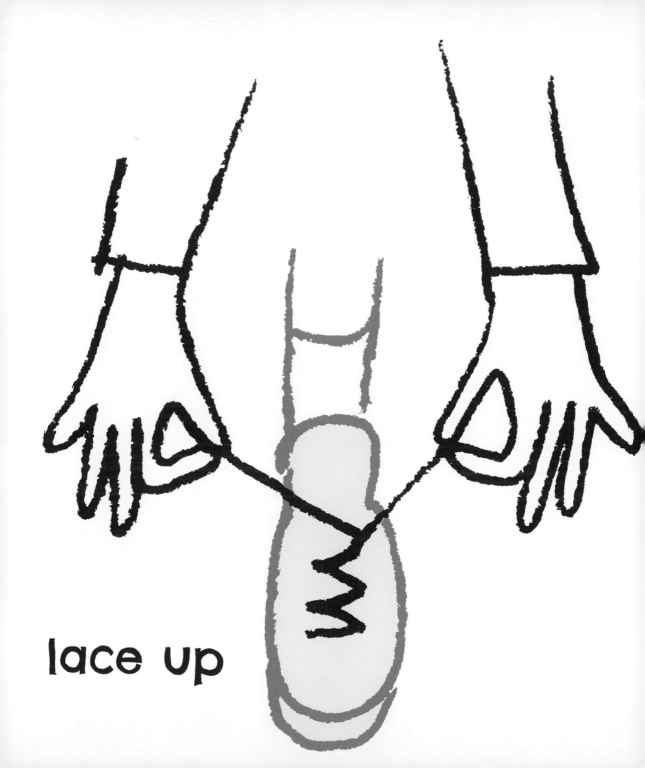

lace up

button up

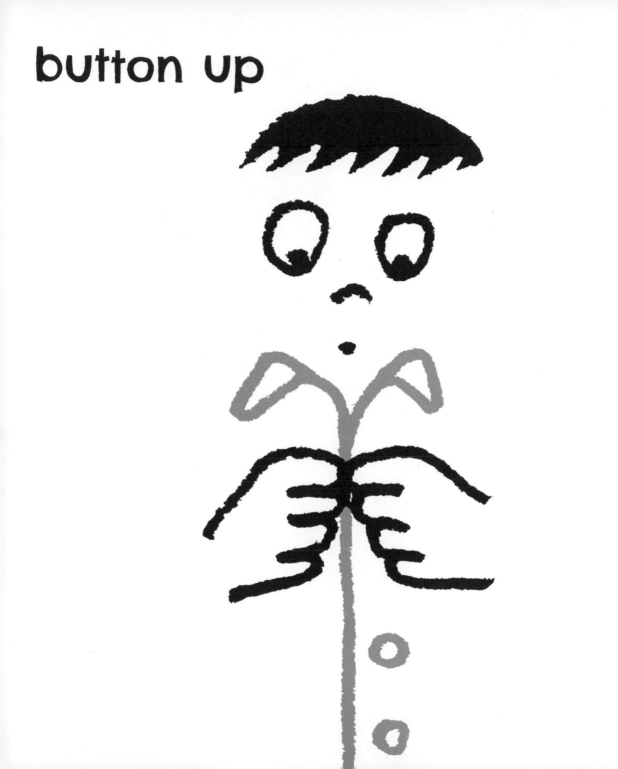

play

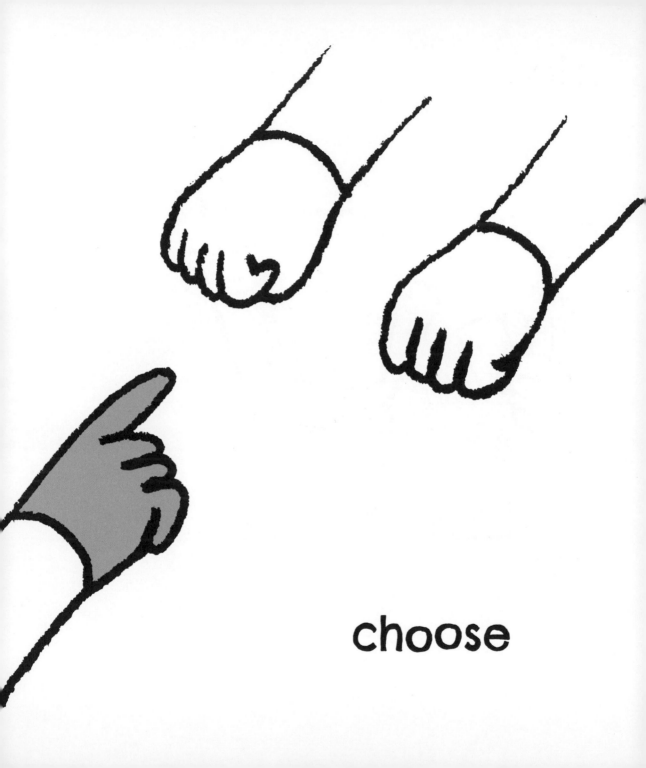

choose

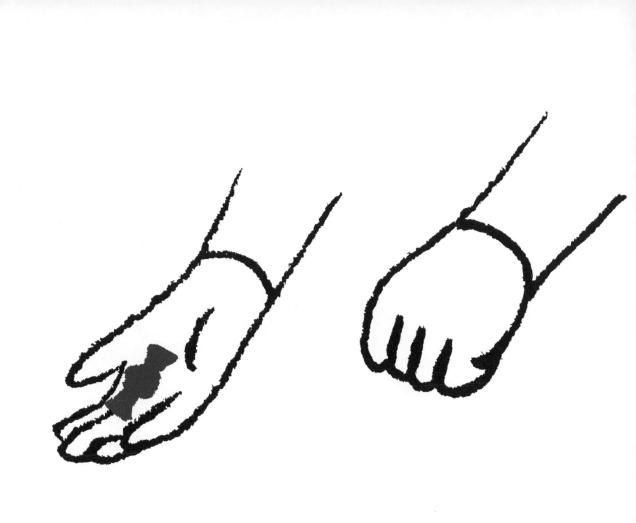

find

give

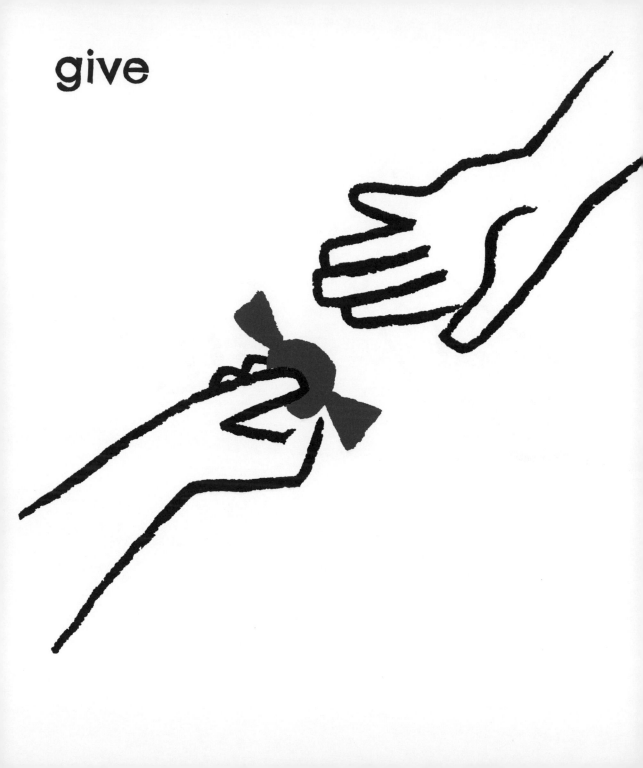

paint

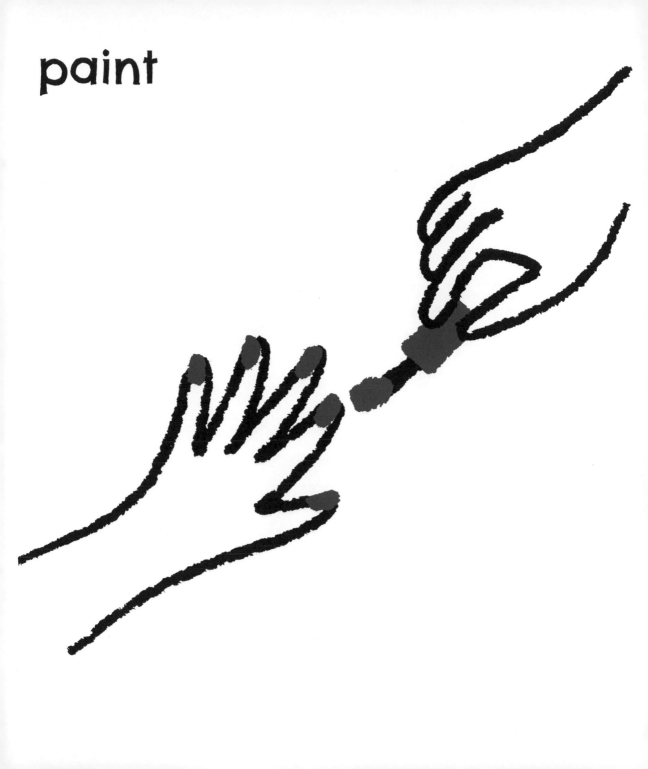

brush
your hair

make a face

dig

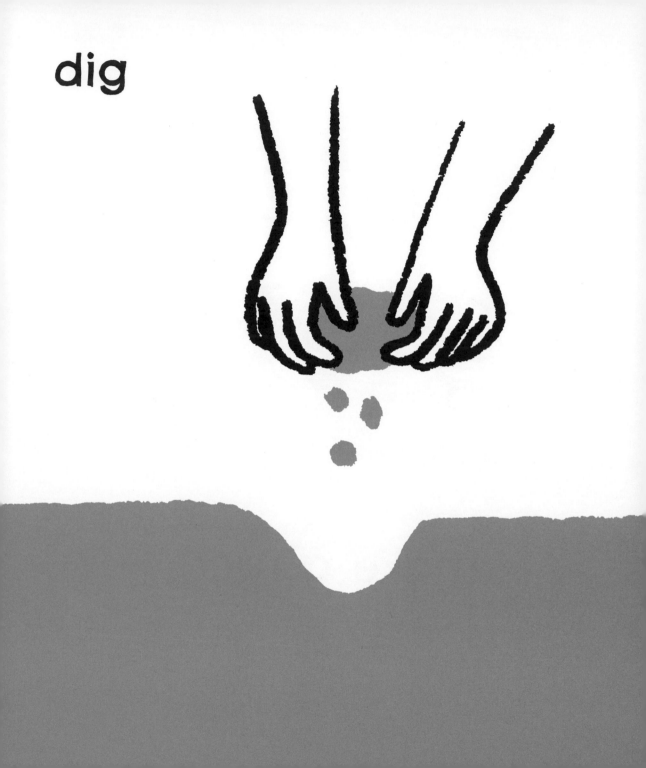

SOW

water

pick

eat

taste

cry

blow your nose

slice

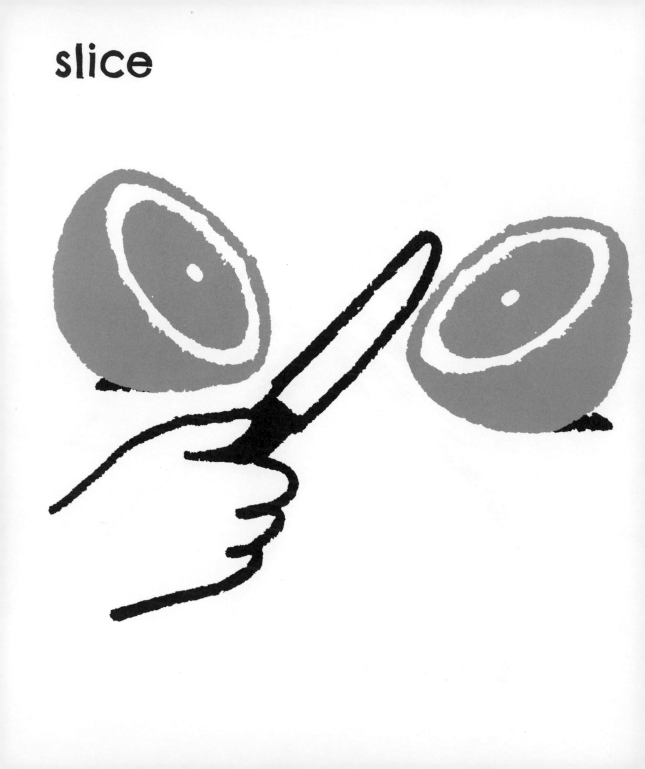

squeeze

serve

cheers!

drink

call

make music

whistle

make a bridge

admire

hold on to

set free

offer

thin out

marry

make happy

it flies

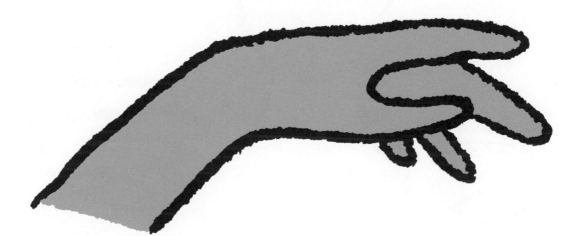

hit

heal

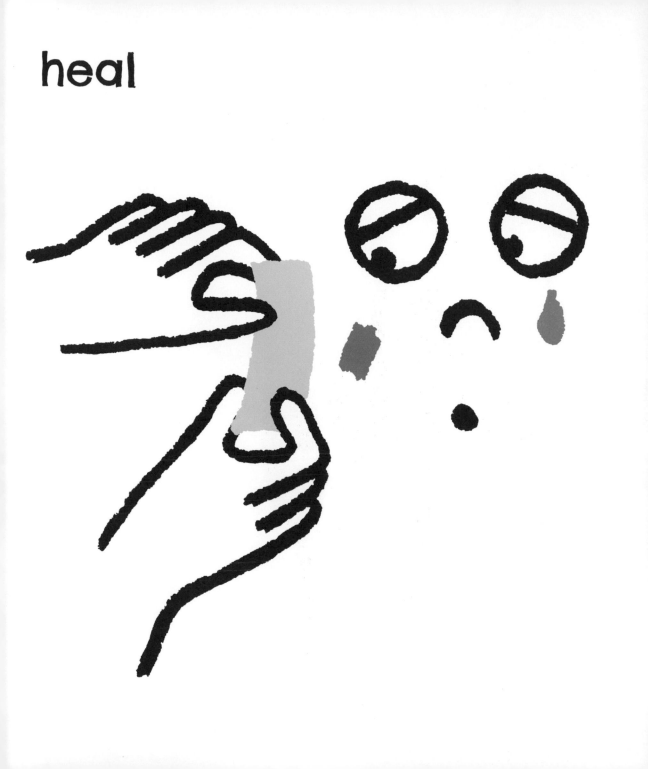

hush!

show

yawn

sleep

turn off